Make a New Friend in Jesus

PassAlong Arch® Books help you share Jesus with friends close to you and with children all around the world!

When you've enjoyed this story, pass it along to a friend. When your friend is finished, mail this book to the address below. Concordia Gospel Outreach promises to deliver your book to a boy or girl somewhere in the world to help him or her learn about Jesus.

Myself

My name _____

My address _____

_____

My PassAlong Friend

My name _____

My address _____

_____

When you're ready to give your PassAlong Arch® Book to a new friend who doesn't know about Jesus, mail it to

Concordia Gospel Outreach
3547 Indiana Avenue
St. Louis, MO 63118

PassAlong Series

God's Good Creation
Noah's Floating Zoo
Baby Moses' River Ride
Moses and the Freedom Journey
Journey to the Promised Land
David and the Dreadful Giant
Jonah's Fishy Adventure
Daniel in the Dangerous Den
Baby Jesus, Prince of Peace
Jesus Stills the Storm
Jesus and Jairus' Little Girl
Jesus' Big Picnic
Jesus and the Little Children
Jesus and the Grumpy Little Man
God's Easter Plan
Peter and the Biggest Birthday

1 2 3 4 5 6 7 8 9 10   04 03 02 01 00 99 98 97 96 95

David
and the
Dreadful Giant

1 Samuel 16–17 for Children

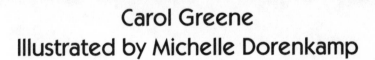

Carol Greene
Illustrated by Michelle Dorenkamp

SAINT LOUIS

An old man now, my thoughts go back
To days when I was young;
To great adventures I have had,
To all the songs I've sung.

For I've been strong and I've been weak;
I've lived through storms and calms.
But God has always been with me.
To Him I've sung my psalms.

"He sings pretty well too!"

With seven brothers I grew up
In little Bethlehem.
They thought that I was just a kid,
Not half as good as them.

And while they did important work,
The sheep I had to tend.
But every day I felt my God
His blessings on me send.

He helped me find the greenest grass
And water cool and pure.
When lion or bear attacked my flock,
He made me strong and sure.

So in those green and happy days,
I learned to sing and play
My prayers to that Good Shepherd who
Leads shepherds on their way.

"Lions? Bears? Help!!"

The Lord's my Shepherd, I'll not want;
He makes me down to lie
In pastures green; He leadeth me
The quiet waters by."

"What a very good shepherd the Lord must be."

Then one day Father called me home
And, right out of the blue,
The prophet Samuel said, "Son,
The Lord has chosen you."

I bowed my head; he poured some oil.
It was the strangest thing—
Instead of herding sheep, I would
Be Israel's next king!

"That's a big promotion!"

At that time Saul ruled Israel,
But he had left God's way.
An evil spirit troubled him,
And I was asked to play.

It seemed my harp could soothe poor Saul.
The evil left him then.
God's Spirit filled my songs. I knew
He'd blessed me once again.

"Saul definitely should not have left God's way."

M y soul He doth restore again
And me to walk doth make
Within the paths of righteousness,
E'en for His own name's sake."

Now Israel fought the Philistines.
Three of my brothers fought.
But when I came with food for them,
Their army seemed distraught.

"A giant fights for the Philistines,"
I heard a soldier say.
"He's ten feet tall, Goliath is.
He taunts us every day."

"That's a lot of giant!"

I wandered off to see King Saul.
"I'll fight that giant," I said.
"God helped me kill the lions and bears.
The giant will soon be dead."

"Well, wear my armor then," said Saul.
It almost crushed my bones.
"I'd rather use my sling," I said—
"Just that and five smooth stones."

"I hope David knows what he's doing."

Yea, though I walk in death's dark vale,
  Yet will I fear no ill;
  For Thou art with me, and Thy rod
  And staff me comfort still."

So out I went to meet the giant.
Goliath stared, then sneered.
"What's this?" he roared "a little boy
Too young to grow a beard?

"Fight me," he said, "and I'll turn you
Into a toothsome feast.
You'll end up dinner, my fine lad,
For every bird and beast."

"That Goliath
is no fun
at all."

I come in God's good name," I said,
And slipped one small smooth stone
Into my sling and raised my arm.
WhurrUP! That stone was thrown.

KaBOOM! He went down like a tree,
And though he looked quite dead,
I grabbed his sword and, just in case,
Chopped off Goliath's head.

My table Thou hast furnished
    In presence of my foes;
    My head Thou dost with oil anoint,
    And my cup overflows."

"Yes, God loves David all right!"

The Philistines got nervous then
And tried to run away.
But our brave soldiers followed and
Killed many more that day.

The king was pleased. The people cheered.
"Praise David!" folks all cried.
But I knew praise belonged to God,
For He fought by my side.

"With God on your side, I guess you can do anything."